FINDING WORDS OF
Power

BRIAN ROSCOE

FINDING WORDS OF POWER
COPYRIGHT © 2021 BY BRIAN ROSCOE

All rights reserved. No part of this publication may be reproduced, distributed, or transmitted in any form or by any means, including photocopying, recording, or other electronic or mechanical methods, without the prior written permission of the author, except in the case of brief quotations embodied in critical reviews and certain other noncommercial uses permitted by copyright law.

The content of this book is for general informational purposes only. It is not meant to be used, nor should it be used, to diagnose or treat any medical condition or to replace the services of your physician or other healthcare provider. The advice and strategies contained in the book may not be suitable for all readers.

Neither the author, publisher, nor any of their employees or representatives guarantees the accuracy of information in this book or its usefulness to a particular reader, nor are they responsible for any damage or negative consequence that may result from any treatment, action taken, or inaction by any person reading or following the information in this book.

For permission requests or to contact the author, visit:
brianroscoeauthor.com

ISBN-13: 978-1-957348-10-0

PRINTED IN THE UNITED STATES OF AMERICA

THE ART OF FINDING YOUR WORDS, FINDING YOUR INFINITE POWER
The infinite power statements moving through words

Yes, words. Both singular in their form and use, as well as together in their infinite combinations. Words are the stuff that Power Statements come alive through! Vitally important to our world, our evolution, and our growth, words are deeply inspired gifts to us. Depending on the version, even in the Bible it says something like, "In the beginning was the Word, and the Word was with God, and the Word was God." Well, that's quite the statement, and proof enough for me that words hold power. There's got to be a reason behind a statement like that.

Think about it. It's through this miracle of words that we express ourselves, through words that we try to expand our understanding of creation. It's words that help us move our thoughts into the world, words that help us create a profound ability to communicate with one another, and it's through our words that we build pictures in our own minds and in the minds of others that inspire a deep connection with being alive. Now isn't that all part of being connected to this miracle of words?

I've always felt that it's truly miraculous that we're able to connect to and interact with one another through a language of words. The complexity of it all really shocks me—the ability to push air through our windpipes and come up with sounds that have so much meaning and potential behind them, not to mention all the gestures and body movements suggesting words and depicting communication. Language is an amazing, precious gift of our human experience, to be valued and not to be taken for granted. What we do with our words can be spectacular, or, if we choose, can cause horrendous pain. Our words are not to be trifled with. They're to be honored and used with respect, and one of the many ways we can do this is with our Power Statements.

Look for your Power Statements through any avenue of communication available: simple words, simple phrases, quotes, songs, magazines, books, poems, prayers, meditations. And do it through whatever reliable source or medium you want. What's important is that you look, and that what you find has heart.

Pay attention to the more ineffable Power Statements of simply being present—the power found in the new-now. These practices may not require our spoken words, but they will naturally inspire them. Consider things like meditation, prayer, or even the simple quiet while sitting in the woods or during a sunset. As you participate in these, before, during, and afterward, pay attention to the words that naturally come forward, let yourself be surprised by the quotes and poems you synchronistically find, and the ideas that seem to spontaneously present themselves. This is your listening heart at work, lining up your life so that what you need to grow is always given the opportunity to be noticed. **So be sure to take a note!**

And let the limit of your Power Statement subject only be limited by your infinite imagination. Pay attention to the statements that are cultivated through taking care of yourself, to Power Statements on the power of intention, personal volition, expressions of love, and self-love, to Power Statements held in our actions, doing and caring for yourself, doing for others, the intention held in life, the Power Statements of self-care: exercise, meditation, healthcare, diet, creating healthy relationships, learning strong communication. All these Power Statement will naturally evolve into a language of description and movement through you. Remember them, and, again, take a note so you can remember them and build on their strength.

Open up to and explore what's already in your environment:

- What movies, literature, music, podcasts, or programming do you already have, listen to, and love because of the messages they have?

- Write down what strikes you. Grab any kind of book, especially one like *Inspirational Espresso*, as you flip through magazines, comic books, health flyers, newspapers. You can find a ton of inspiring and growth-oriented ideas to draw from just floating around. These publications are meant to inspire the mind in some direction. It's up to you where you go with it.

- Talking with friends is an awesome source of inspiration and wisdom. Ask them what they're drawn to, who they admire, what they're inspired by, and where their greatest growth comes from. They might not have an answer right away, and think you're a little weird, but they likely already knew that, and that's probably why they love you. But questions like these are the ones people walk away with and think about, and they tend to encourage conversations later.

- Pay attention to the phrases that strike you when you're watching a movie, listening to the radio or a podcast. Again, someone has put some real thought into these productions, they're meant to catch your attention.

- And, of course, the internet is flooded with inspirational sayings, not to mention its share of negativity. So search smart, look for your concepts of mindfulness, wisdom, exercises and techniques of health, meditation, and heart-centered inspiration. Explore and find your tools

- As far as the negativity, wish them peace and let it show you what you don't want to involve yourself with. That's a huge lesson within itself.

EXPLORING

**What ideas in this abundant world
tugs on the strings of your heart?
What speaks to you?
What drives you to act?**

What concepts of living, ideas of the spirit, interests of the mind and intellect are you drawn to in this abundant world? Where does your heart consistently and stubbornly point you, and what does it draw you into despite the temptations of a distracting and often misleading mind? How does your heart try to pull you from the shell you've surrounded yourself with, and away from all the dogma held in your human opinions? Can you hear the whispering heart as it attempts to influence the soul of your life?

This is where you look for your Power Statements. It's in this place, within the core of who you are, that you authentically present yourself to yourself, and open to the world, paving your own road to re-discover yourself. This is you giving your pure light to what's happening inside of and through you.

Explore and nurture your heart. Open to what's moving through you, open to the wisdom and truth that asks for expression. Pay attention to the internal communication that takes place beyond the mouth, and give language to the light of being alive.

What are you drawn to? How do you best learn and absorb? By reading, hearing the spoken word, visually, watching an example? It's likely your go-to mode of exploring the world. So pay attention to that. Use it, but don't neglect the other avenues of exploration, because there's huge value in those approaches, too.

- What concepts draw you in?
- What ideas touch you?
- What surprises you about this life?
- What ideas are you scared to explore, but curious to understand?
- Who were you before you were born to this world?
- Ask questions about things that shock you. The secrets. The nonconforming ideas in the world.
- What uniqueness in this abundant world calls for your exploration?
- What uniqueness do you bring to this world—a wonder already held within you?

Explore and stay open to all your questions of life, your desires for knowledge, all your curiosities, and confusion. Explore all the movements in your mind and take note, and then explore for the answers, and learn what feeds your heart.

WORDS EXPRESS ENERGY

Words are energy. Period. They produce internal experiences for us, delivering the power to hurt and to heal. Words open us up to the miracle of communication, and they rock our world every day, in all kinds of ways. Words are powerful. Use them as an extension of yourself, to project your truth and to expand your heart. Use your miracle language with honor and respect. Use it to help, not hinder, and use it to expand life, not suppress it. Words have energy.

We put a lot of effort into life, investigating our human experience in all its forms. Words are a huge part of it. We're all busy exploring our communication, various forms of literature and media, quotes, words, interactions of all kinds, and the human meaning behind all these words is a wonderful exercise for the heart. Participating in life with our words, whether written, spoken, signed, read or listened to, is like saying thank you to the universe, thank you to God, thank you for the gift of being alive, the privilege of being human. What an adventure!

Finding what's important to you, what speaks to you, what inspires your heart, is not always easy. Sometimes, it requires a little exploration. Below is a list of potential words that might whisper to you. Find the ones that touch deepest within, the words and concepts that call for your attention, or even the ones that create resistance in you. Pay attention to what inspires joy, pain, laughter, or tears, because it's in that pop of emotion that you see what needs to be worked on and explored within.

> *"Surely, life is not merely a job, an occupation; life is something extraordinarily wide and profound, it is a great mystery, a vast realm in which we function as human beings."*
> – Jiddu Krishnamurti

EXPLORING WORDS FROM OTHER LANGUAGES

Exploring words can be fun! No, really. It can be, especially words from different cultures and languages. If you want to spice up the journey of being human a bit, consider exploring words from other languages. All languages have their limitations, and English is no exception. It certainly has its drawbacks when it comes to finding precise words that express complex emotions and the concepts surroudning being human. Other languages and cultures have words for our human experience that English may not have developed. These other languages have explored and developed words for feelings and our connection with spirit and heart that are uniquely authentic to them, and worthy of our curious examination.

So often the meaning behind a word draws a picture in your mind that creates a feeling you just want to hold and remember—to nurture the concept within yourself and make it part of your world. So if it's in you, go ahead and explore the words and phrases invented by different languages, tribes, and cultures. You'll find that we all think about the same stuff, it's just that different groups develop more expressive words around different experiences. Explore, see how others see and describe our common human adventure—*life.*

Following is a list of words from a variety of cultures, words from around the world with no exact English equivalent. Each one is accompanied by a small discussion explaining their origin, the intent, and the meaning of the word. Some are quite thought-provoking and inspiring, they might even motivate you to explore a little further on your own.

Personally, I love the creative differences of cultural greetings. They're all so unique in their intention and message. I am always intrigued at how we see one another. So that's what I'm going to start with!

So many cultures around the world regard greeting one another as something far more than just a pleasantry, a simple hello, how-are-ya passing platitude. Greeting happens from the heart and soul of who we are. It opens us to the opportunities of simply touching and being touched by one another with a grace and honor. A gift deserved by all.

Sawubona (Zulu)

The Zulu greeting "sawubona" means "we see you." They use "we" instead of "I" because they believe that their eyes are connected to their ancestors' eyes. The other person would respond with "ngikhona," which means "I am here," or "yabo, sawubona," meaning "yes, we see you, too." By letting them know that you see them, you are inviting them to participate in your life with deep witnessing.

Zdraveite (Bulgarian)

This word is derived from the Bulgarian word "zdrave," which means "health." When people say hello in Bulgaria, they are wishing the other person to stay safe and healthy.

Aloha (Hawaiian)

According to a folk etymology, the word "aloha" is a compound of the Hawaiian word "alo," meaning "presence," "face," and "share," and "ha," meaning "essence of life." It is a greeting said from the heart with feelings of mutual regard and affection, love, peace, and compassion, with no obligation to receive anything in return.

Shalom (Hebrew)

"Shalom alechem" is a Hebrew greeting meaning "peace be upon you." The response being "alechem shalom" or "unto you, peace." This form of greeting is traditional among Jews throughout the world. The plural form is used even when addressing one person because one greets both the body and the soul. "Shalom" also connotes completeness, wholeness, health, peace, welfare, safety, soundness, tranquility, prosperity, perfectness, fullness, rest, harmony, and the absence of agitation or discord. When you say "shalom," you are wishing someone a wonderful life with everything that shalom represents!

Namasté (nah-mah-stay) (Hindu)

In the West, it's often heard at the end of yoga classes, and as we dig deeper into the intention and meaning behind it, we see that "namasté" is a salutation of respect and reverence. It literally translates to "I bow to you," however, in traditional Hinduism, it means "I bow to the divine in you" or, "the divine in me bows to the divine in you." "Namaste" can be spoken with or without the prayerful gesture of bringing ones palms together in front of the body (the palms and all ten fingers touch one another, with the thumbs joining in front of the heart space or brow) and gently bowing while speaking the greeting/blessing.

Hongi (Māori)

The traditional Māori greeting is called "the hongi." It's a greeting performed between two people by pressing their noses and often their foreheads together as they share a breath. In the hongi, the "ha" (breath of life) is exchanged in a symbolic show of unity. The greeting and exchange of breath can also be followed by a handshake. With this exchange, one is no longer considered simply a visitor, rather one of the people of the land.

Wabi Sabi (Japanese)

This term refers to finding the beauty in the imperfections of life and accepting that everything is constantly changing. The idea of wabi sabi comes from Buddhist teachings on impermanence, suffering, and emptiness or absence of self-nature.

In Japan, the concept of wabi sabi is seen as a universal view of life, centered on the acceptance of its inherent transience and imperfection. It describes an essence of beauty in life that is imperfect, impermanent, and incomplete. There's a rustic quality to objects described with the phrase "wabi sabi." A roughness, asymmetrical look, simple in nature and natural in appearance.

Modern use of the term connotes rustic simplicity, freshness or quietness, adding a uniqueness and elegance to the a beauty of an object, often seen as a serenity that comes with age. It can be applied to both natural and human-made objects, or understated elegance.

Firgun and Mudita

"Firgun" is a hebrew word, very similar to the concept of "mudita" (Sanskrit and Pali). They both denote the feeling of sympathetic or unselfish joy, or joy in the good fortune or success of others with a good heart and without jealousy. Jealousy and envy, as well as the German phrase "Schadenfreude" (when you take joy in someone else's misfortune), would be considered the opposite of "firgun" and "mudita."

Hygge (HEW-gə or HOO-ga) (both Danish and Norwegian)

Hygge is a warm, cozy feeling that washes over you; it needs to be experienced to be known. It's considered a quality of cosiness and good-natured warmth that inspires a feeling of contentment or wellbeing. The Danish consider it a defining characteristic of their culture.

It's a little confusing, but, in short, Hygge may originate from the word "hug," taken from an old Danish word meaning "to give courage, comfort, joy." In Old Norse, the word "hugr" later becames "hug," and means the soul, mind, and consciousness.

So then, can it be that a hug is an embrace of the soul, mind, and consciousness that's meant to help us bring courage, comfort, and joy to one another?

Meraki, (mer-a-ki) (modern Greek)

Meraki means doing something with a deep sense of spirit. It's used to describe what happens when you leave a piece of yourself (your soul, creativity, or love) in your work. When you love doing anything so much that you put "something of yourself" into what you're doing, it's a true labor of love. *Hmmm, sounds like writing to me... What a great title!* And am I stretching too far by thinking that it kind of sounds like the word "miracle?"

Nunchi (Korean)

"Nunchi" literally translates as "eye measure." It's having the ability to determine others' moods, resulting in knowing what to say or not to say or do in a given situation simply by being in their presence and/or listening to them. Nunchi is having the ability to communicate through body language, gestures and intuition, it's the subtle art of listening on a higher level to others and being able to gauge their state of wellbeing as you relate to them. In Korea, people can be considered as having different qualities of nunchi: a high level of or an absence of nunchi, or even quick witted nunchi, are typical observations. In the West, this might be seen as having a particular level of emotional intelligence, or even as being empathic.

Strikhedonia (Greek)

This is the pleasure of being able to say, "To hell with it!" I actually love this word, not as an active aggression or bad feeling toward anything, but as an act of freeing oneself from old thinking that needs to be let go of.

Talk about being in the joy of finally being able to let go of something we may have held as a burden for a very long time. How wonderful and empowering it is to the heart when we can do it without resentment or taking it personally.

Gunnen (Dutch)

Similar to "firgun" and "mudita," "gunnen" is the experience of finding happiness in someone else's happiness because your love for them is so great. It has also been explained as the act of joyfully giving someone the chance of a positive experience, even if it results in you not having it.

Oodal (Tamil)

"Oodal" is the fake anger that couples tease each other with. Almost like a light form of banter, it's that exaggerated, often melodramatic anger and sulking between lovers when they purposefully let themselves get offended (usually over something inconsequential) in an attempt to get the other to apologize first. It's done with affection and it's a way to playfully strengthen bonds.

Yugen (Japanese)

The Japanese have many important concepts

of aesthetics as they relate to life and art, often one in the same. Yūgen is one of many worth exploring.

Yūgen is an awareness of the universe that leaves you with emotions too deep and mysterious for words. Similar to the definition of the word "ineffable," "yūgen" refers to feelings and ideas too great or extreme to be expressed or described in words.

> Using the idea of yūgen in writing:
> *"To contemplate the flight of wild geese seen and lost among the clouds."*
> -Zeami Motokiyo

Yūgen describes a depth of appreciation for this experience of life, one that sees and allows us to be one with all the ineffable and profound beauty of the universe as it presents itself, as well as the sad beauty of human suffering.

Dadirri (Australian aboriginal term)

"Dadirri" is a deep, spiritual act of quiet, reflective and respectful listening—a still awareness within. It's a tuning in, a reconnection experience with the specific aim to remember our deeper understanding of the beauty of nature. Dadirri recognizes the inner spirit that calls us to reflection and contemplation of the immense wonders of this creation.

Sukha (Sanskrit)

"Sukha" is genuine, lasting happiness, independent of circumstances. In Sanskrit and Pali, "suhka" means an authentic state of happiness, pleasure, ease, or bliss that has a lasting quality, compared to "preya" which is more of a transient pleasure. So "sukha" refers more to happiness with a comfort and a settled sense of ease to it. Regarding the function of our bodies, sukha means that everything is working together harmoniously. Here, comfort and ease may not always be appropriate descriptive words. Better definitions might be physical balance, homeostasis, and wellbeing. It's a kind of body equanimity.

Orenda (Iroquois)

"Orenda" is the Iroquois name for a spiritual energy inherent in people and their environment. Even storms are said to possess orenda—just stand outside and watch as a storm approaches. Feel its presence. It's a collective power of nature's energies through the living energy of all natural objects, animate and inanimate. It's an extraordinary invisible power believed to live in varying degrees in all animate and inanimate natural objects. It's a transmissible spiritual energy capable of being exerted according to the will of its possessor. A strong connection exists between prayers and songs and orenda: through song, a bird, shaman, all put forth orenda. Orenda describes the power of our volition as we relate to ourselves and our world—the ability of the human will to change the world in the face of the powerful forces surrounding them.

So that's my list. And make no mistake about it, there's a world of words, concepts, greetings, and forms of love to choose from on this planet! Make a list of your favorite words that you might like to have in your life, or even try and work into your vocabulary. Try and own them, really explore their meanings so you resonate with their message.

> *Note:* To understand the essence of a word doesn't require you to memorize it or even use it. Simply having knowledge of it enables you to, in some way, embody it, to make it part of your life. Just be aware of its essence, its existence, and use that knowledge to support your life.

FINDING WORDS OF *Power*

JUMPING INTO THE GAME

Here's a little direction for finding your Power Statements. Try this thinking exercise to help you explore, build, and refine your list to draw from. As you ask yourself some of the simple questions below, open yourself up to all the possible directions you can go with them. Remember, it's an exercise of personal exploration. Give yourself permission to let anything and anyone be a potential catalyst to finding the triggers of inspiration hidden within you.

Do your best to answer some of these questions. It helps to have a pen and paper or note-taking device in hand. You can try and answer them all at once or just approach one a week. You can scan them all and just pick out the ones that strike your fancy, or hit the ones that make you nervous. It's your journey, do it how you want. But when an idea, word, or person pops in your head, it helps to write it down so you can explore when you want without having to memorize everything (which, in my mind, is just way too much work)!

- **What subjects do you love to talk about?**
  What feeds you? What can you not stop talking about once you get rolling? What do you fearlessly talk about with your most comfortable, trusted, and connected friend? Heart stuff? Body stuff? Intellectual concepts? A mixture of all of them? Do your best to make a list, write them down.

- **What and who inspires you?**
  Anything at all? Health concepts? Creativity, art, writing, invention? The motivation of others? Bravery? Courage?

Children? The Olympics? The Special Olympics? People stepping beyond adversity and making choices of strength in life? Those who have recognized their special gifts and embraced them? The story of an average Joe expanding past his/her social programing and finding their truth? People taking care of one another? Great feats of heroism? Little gifts of great love? Exploring any of these ideas or people can shed light on what it is to feed your own heart. Your time is well spent looking into all kinds of concepts, ideas, and people that reflect your own heart in some way.

- **What subjects are you hesitant to discuss with others and what do you just hate to talk about?**

  Is there fear around it, and do you find yourself making yourself small because of it? Take a look at the things that scare or anger you—they're the subjects worth exploring, worth looking for the *why* behind them, and the wisdom hiding within the healing of our response to them.

- **What concepts tend to create judgment in your mind?**

  Judgment. Pay attention here, peel your judgment apart, dissect it. Wherever our judgment pulls on us hardest reveals something of our greatest lessons. So don't avoid looking at the things that make you feel ugly. They are teachers for the eager student. There's always an opportunity for healing where judgment is addressed. We can always find wisdom and truth when we move beyond our judgment.

- **Who do you love? Who do you really really not love? And why?**

  Just open up to the why, the reasons, the inspiration behind the good feeling as well as the repulsion, and write down the thinking that creates what you believe you feel.

- **What do you have the courage to think about when no one is around?**

  What are the secrets of you, the freedom of the heart as it moves through you? What are the very personal messages here, or the healing being summoned through you?

- **What do you "wish" you could talk about freely?**

  Are there "taboo" subjects that we unnecessarily fear, or are there things that need to be explored and healed within?

- **Loved by society or not, which figures inspire you?**

  Look for the *why*. It's okay if it's Mother Theresa or Napoleon. But why? What is the strength or the truth these people inspire in your mind and heart?

- **Alive or dead, made-up or real, who are your greatest heroes?**

  Look for the *why*.

- **What feeds your heart, your mind, your most intense as well as your mildest interests in life?**

  Touch on what holds your attention—anything and everything if you want. This is your unique life, your *Power Statement Logbook*, put absolutely anything you want on your list of potentials for exploration and inspiration!

Take your time. Explore the words and concepts behind the questions that grab you. Give yourself the freedom to explore beyond what's easily seen, allow any boundaries to fade, and get into the grit of who you are.

All your answers, your words, or your phrases give you something to draw from. They're fuel for the journey, things to look at, potentials for inspiration, reasons for change, and opportunities for growth. Without judgment or emotional attachment, explore your concepts, the people, or ideas that touch you. Open yourself to the good, the bad, and the ugly as you explore the nature of your relationship to the human condition. Even exploring your most negative concept is an exercise for potential healing when you do it with heart. When we're open, we can find ways that help us move away from our negativity or toxicity around it. Because if you know where the pain is, it's easier to treat the wound.

Make a list of things that really turn your gears in life—the people and concepts that really twists your piggies. You're looking for the ideas that spark your higher interest and touch your heart in some way. Refine the words that feed you and see what sticks, let them frame a picture in your mind you can draw from. Grab some paper, or your phone, and take a note. Create a list you can build on over time, you can get rid of it whenever you want, come back to it whenever the time is right, keep it in your desk, or just hold it in your pocket as your reminder. It's your personal freedom list—just do your best to make it work for you.

This is an example of how I explored *silence* **and** *quiet*—**how I dug into a word and concept that's meaningful to me:**
In my world, sitting quietly holds a lot of importance. It moves me, and I've always known that it helps me reset—to somehow freshen myself. Admittedly, I never really understood exactly what that need was about. I just knew that quiet and solitude was good for me, and it felt important to nurture.

It wasn't until I explored what others had to say about silence and quiet and what it meant to them that I was able to get a firmer grasp on it for myself. I explored quotes, read poems, listened to ideas, found and considered the antonyms and synonyms, read the book *Quiet* by Susan Cain, and simply took time to study and absorb the deeper words around this inner place of solitude I so loved. My research helped me uniquely define it for myself. Their words gave me permission to expand into my quiet, to appreciate my intuitive need for time spent in the presence and wisdom of silence.

Below are some quotes that I connected with. They showed me I was not alone, and, really, that I'm in pretty good company. These are a few examples of many that helped me cultivate a greater understanding and acceptance of my need for solitude and quiet. Quotes like these helped explain why I felt like I derive such strength and rejuvenation through silence and meditation. Not surprisingly, Albert Einstein and Rumi were favorites.

> *"The monotony and solitude of a quiet life stimulates the creative mind."*
> -Albert Einstein

"Silence is the sleep that nourishes wisdom."
–Francis Bacon

*"Listen to silence.
It has much to say."*
–Rumi

"Silence is a source of great strength."
–Lao Tzu

"Silence, healing."
–Heraclitus

"Solitude is a catalyst for innovation."
–Susan Cain

*"The quieter you become,
the more you are able to hear."*
–Rumi

> "Muddy water is best cleared
> by leaving it alone."
> -Alan Watts

> "I never found the companion that was so
> companionable as solitude. We are for the most
> part more lonely when we go abroad among men
> than when we stay in our chambers."
> -Henry David Thoreau

> "Everything has its wonders, even darkness
> and silence, and I learn whatever state I
> am in, therein to be content."
> -Helen Keller

> "I think 99 times and find nothing. I stop
> thinking, swim in silence, and the truth
> comes to me."
> -Albert Einstein

I also searched the antonyms and synonyms for silence and quiet. Here are some simple words that I felt a connection with.

Synonyms: calm, peaceful, soft, close, still
Antonyms: clamorous, noisy, agitation, unruly

Quiet: The Power of Introverts in a World That Can't Stop Talking
by Susan Cain

I found a friend in this book. It helped me to see and more deeply understand myself, to embrace why I walked through life in my unique way. Quiet helped me understand myself and be myself. The author had found greater understanding for her own world, and through a peak into her process, it helped me do the same for my own world.

I also saw Ms. Cain speak some years back at a venue in Grand Rapids. Being in the presence of someone who has done so much thinking on and research about the importance of following our need for quiet was validating in a way books could not impart. There was an energetic exchange that comes from being in the same room with someone who connects with your heart. This was another link in the chain of accepting myself and finding my greater balance.

Note: You don't always have to go to such extremes with the concepts you want to explore. Sometimes a simple quote might suffice, or finding an idea that the mind can gain a little understanding through. With quiet and silence, I simply found myself drawn to and immersed in the subject and its power, so I went with it. And I'm still drawn in. I still find myself exploring it often. It seems like there's always a new bit of gold to be found—a little more truth to be had for the journey.

SIMPLE POWER STATEMENTS

Simple Power Statements are just that. They're the easy to understand words, phrases, and ideas that present a truth that extends beyond their simplicity. They help us build a framework within that creates a structure of strength, one that only requests and requires the attention of the heart.

Create a list of your simplest Power Statements.
Examples:
"I am..."
"I am love."
"Allow"
"Listen"
"Listen to the whisper."

FINDING WORDS OF *Power*

-
-
-
-
-
-
-
-
-

LISTENING FOR POWER STATEMENTS
hearing with your heart

A patient of mine, Bob, mentioned that his wife said to him, out of pure frustration for the tension they always seemed to be feeling in their lives, "And this! This is supposed to be the best time of our lives?"

It was a profound statement for him to hear, and he held on to the intention behind the question. As soon as he heard it, he knew it was meant to direct him. It turned into his Power Statement at that moment. Just the question of how to spend the best-time-of-life money (the retirement fund) caused him into re-evaluate the way he was living, where he was putting his importance. It was a hint received from his wife through a frustrated off-hand comment. But it meant more to Bob. He heard the message loud and clear. It was at that point Bob decided he was going to make whatever time they had left in this world worth it; that the rest of their lives would be "the best time of their lives," and he commented that it always should've been.

They didn't have much money, but they both more than made up for their lack of finances with their attitudes. They set their minds and hearts up to see the abundance of life surrounding them every day. They knew they had everything they needed to be happy, and when they did feel stressed, they chose to reevaluate their thinking, they looked for the solutions, antidotes, and qualities of thinking that helped move them into a state of wellbeing that reflected "the best time of their lives."

Bob was listening. And both he and Jackie

caught wind of that little epiphany flying by, and they used it. They grabbed on to some inspired truth, found through playfully whining with each other about life, and they made it work for them—they made their lesson work for them. Life is a temporary thing, and we all have just one shot to run around the track. They found themselves asking: *Why not make this the best time of our lives? What are we waiting for? Why not embrace each of life's moments as new, fresh, and wonderful whenever we get the opportunity? Why not live in the abundance life is offering us right now?* And they lived a little more happily ever after, with plenty more lessons to come… because life is how it is.

We hear first with our *heart*, it helps us feed our *mind*.

Your heart is always paying attention to what's happening. Around and within you, your heart is listening. It hears all the rumbles of life as it flows through you, it brings a spark of attention to what moves you, and it communicates with its unmistakable whisper what's most important for you to know in life. Your heart's always listening, and it only asks you to listen back for its quiet wisdom.

"And the day came when the risk to remain tight in a bud was more painful than the risk it took to blossom."

-Anais Nin

www.ingramcontent.com/pod-product-compliance
Lightning Source LLC
Chambersburg PA
CBHW021432070526
44577CB00001B/170